Table of Contents

Introduction 4
What is the Noom diet? 6
Tips for Noom Diet 6
How does the Noom diet work? 12
Benefits of Noom 13
What can you eat on the Noom diet? 16
Why could the Noom diet work for you? 18
Is there any evidence for its effectiveness? 19
Research into the Noom app 20
Possible risks 21
Healthy recipes for some meals on a Noom Diet 22
    Herbed Chicken Marsala 22
    Lemony Yogurt Pound Cake 24
    Sloppy Joes 25
    Pan-Seared Salmon with Kale and Apple Salad 26
    Lentil Vegetable Soup 28
    Mixed Berries and Banana Smoothie 30
    Breakfast Casserole 31
    Broiled Salmon with Herb Mustard Glaze 32
    Whole30 Bacon and Egg Cups 34
    Slow-Cooker Pork Tacos 35

Vegetable Noodle Soup 37
Angel Food Cake 39
Blueberry Compote 40
Chicken Saltimbocca 41
Spaghetti Squash and Meatballs 43
Buffalo Cauliflower with Blue Cheese Sauce 45
Roasted Cauliflower and Broccoli 47
Tuscan Vegetable Soup 48
Three Bean and Beef Chili 49
Lemon-Garlic Shrimp and Grits 51
Oil and Vinegar Slaw 52
Quinoa Salad 53
Teriyaki Chicken Thighs 54
Shrimp Stir-Fry 55
Low-Cal Fettuccine Alfredo 57
Marinated Chicken Breasts 59
Breakfast Burrito 60
Chia Seed Pudding 61
Healthified Broccoli Cheddar Soup 63
Pork Chops With Apples and Garlic Smashed Potatoes . 64
Hasselback Sweet Potatoes 66
Herb-Marinated Pork Tenderloins 67
Pasta and Beans: Pasta e Fagioli 69

Beef Stir-Fry 71
Gazpacho 72
Green Beans with Lemon and Garlic 74
Healthy Cauliflower Rice 75
Oven "Fries" 76
Roman-Style Chicken 77
Salmon Baked in Foil 79
One-week sample menu 80
Monday 80
Tuesday 81
Wednesday 81
Thursday 81
Friday 82
Saturday 82
Sunday 82
Conclusion 83

Introduction

Noom is a wellness program that is designed to help you live a healthier life by helping you create better habits.

Unlike other weight loss programs that focus just on the physical aspect of losing weight, noom focuses on the mental aspect as well.

Because sometimes losing weight is more than just eating well and being active. Yes those parts a very important, but sometimes it just isn't enough.

For many, struggles with weight loss has a lot to do with personal thoughts and emotions that tend to be barriers.

Which is what makes noom so unique. Their goal is to help you overcome these barriers by helping you become more aware of poor habits and creating better ones.

The Noom diet is a personalized weight loss plan available through the phone app of the same name. The app's creators claim that it helps people reach their personal weight goals.

The Noom app provides its users with a personalized diet plan and access to a health coach.

People can also use the app to record their diet and exercise habits, and to discuss their weight loss journey on Noom's social platform.

If you've put on a few more pounds during lockdown, then don't worry because the Noom diet could help you lose them and you're definitely not the only one. Having to minimise our exercise, and spend much more time near the snack cupboard, it's no wonder many of us feel the need to start cutting back to slim down.

While experienced dieters have turned to famous methods like intermittent fasting and diets such as the 5:2, or plans that rely on one food group like the high protein diet to lose the weight, others are confused about which course could be the best for them. After all, there are so many out there and every one seems to work differently. Some diets are restrictive (like the Fruitarian Diet) and others promise that you can eat still eat all the things you enjoy (see: What is the Sirtfood Diet?)

So, what if you want a new diet plan? One that is loved by millions?

Step forward, the Noom diet. Not only was it the most Googled diet in 2018, but it's been tried by more than 45 million people worldwide. Wondering if it could work for you? Here's everything you need to know…

In this book, we explore the Noom diet and outline the research into its effectiveness.

What is the Noom diet?

The Noom app allows people to self-monitor their weight loss.

Noom is an app designed to help people lose weight, get fit, and stay healthy. It uses a unique traffic light system to rank foods based on how many calories they contain.

"Green" foods such as spinach and broccoli are the least calorie dense, whereas "red" foods contain more calories and should make up less of a portion.

Using these data, the app's creators develop personalized weight loss plans that they claim can help deliver long lasting weight loss results.

To get a personalized weight loss plan, a person will need to purchase a subscription and answer some questions on the Noom website or app. The algorithm will then design a weight loss plan to fit the person's needs.

Shortly after a person logs in for the first time, the app will pair them with an appropriate health coach. The coach will provide relevant dietary information and advice to help the person achieve their weight goals.

Tips for Noom Diet

1. The Noom Food Database

Losing weight is all about making sure you burn more calories than you consume. Knowing this, the best way to make sure you lose weight effectively is to make sure you are tracking the food you eat on a daily basis.

However, we can all agree that this process can be a bit tedious. Not only is it tedious, but it can be a bit difficult knowing what is actually being put into the food you eat, which can also cause you to get poor results.

With noom, they make the process of selecting food so much easier. They let you browse and compare different food options which makes logging your food simple.

Noom has a very large food database with over 3.7 million options to choose from. You can even select the portion sizes that make sense for the actual food item you're selecting. The best part, all this can be done from your fingertips since you will be using your phone.

Also, this is why it's important to be up to date with technological advances. We pretty much do everything from our phones, so being able to accurately log your activity will be key to getting the best results.

I'm sure you're probably thinking that other programs have these features when it comes to meal selection. But what separates noom from all the others?

2. Your Plan Is Created By A Team Of Experts

One thing you have to be careful with, especially when it comes to these fad diets out there, is how the diet plan is created. You want to know that what you're eating is being selected by specialists who understand what it takes to be healthy.

With noom, your diet plan is being selected by a team of nutritionists and registered dietitians. They oversee the food database to make sure users are getting the most accurate information in regards to their diet.

This ensures that everything you log within the app is recorded to help you meet your daily goals. This will give you the confidence to know that you are creating good habits for long term success.

3. Noom Offers Two Types Of Programs

The noom weight loss plan offers both a healthy weight program and the diabetes management program. This will be important when selecting food items as each item is color coded based on those two programs.

Healthy Weight Program – with this program, you will notice that when selecting your food, each item is color coded based on calories, which is key to weight loss.

Everyday you will have a calorie budget, and it's important to make sure that you don't go over it. But you will find that tracking and logging your meals much easier to understand as you work towards your goal...Learn More

Diabetes Management Program – when it comes to those suffering with diabetes, less emphasis will be on calories, and will be more on carbohydrate intake. Management and proper care will be key to successful weight loss.

Having the option for both type of programs allows for users to gain better control and understanding over their weight issues. It also helps that you have a team of experts providing you with sound advice.

4. What Kind Of Foods Can You Eat?

Knowing what to eat is always a hot topic when it comes to figuring out healthy weight loss. People are always wondering what others are eating that allows them to get in such great looking shape.

For some, being consistent and eating the same thing everyday is a good way to go about it. Yes you may say it's boring, and I would agree, but it can be very effective.

But for those not interested in taking the boring route, and would prefer a little variety, the noom diet allows for just that. As long as you stay within your dietary budget of course.

Since weight loss is about burning more calories than you consume, it's important to make sure you stay around your daily calorie goal. And since noom specifies each food item in their database, managing that budget is made simple for you.

So when it comes to knowing what foods you can eat, it really is up to you. As long as you are able to stay around your dietary budget, you can enjoy the foods you like.

5. Personalized Feedback To Keep You On Track

I think one of the coolest things about the noom program is the feedback you get throughout the day. This is especially helpful for those that are in the Noom Diabetes Management Program.

The fact that all food items are color coded based on the program you're on, as you continue to log your food, noom gives feedback for your selections. So making sure you are logging consistently will be important.

As you log your food, noom will keep track of everything and even make suggestions to help improve your meal selections in the future.

For many, this is the exact guidance that is needed to make sure you stay on track. It can be so easy to fall back into poor habits that get in the way of you getting the best results. So having this type of accountability can be a huge boost for your long term health.

6. Noom Isn't...

A diet, but a way of living. With noom, you're not getting some program that's made to last only a few weeks or months. Noom's goal is to make sure you're equipped with the tools and knowledge to keep the weight off for good.

Noom is all about making long-term changes to achieve weight loss goals. Noom's green food list will help you learn which foods are ok to consume based on your calorie budget.

Using colors like, green yellow, and red, you can easily identify which foods will help you reach your weight loss goals.

Now that doesn't mean you can't eat foods that are marked red, it just means you need to be mindful of the foods you're consuming.

Noom will help you develop better eating habits so that eventually you're able to manage your diet without the help of Noom.

7. Make Sure To Watch Your Calorie Intake

Remember that losing weight is all about calories. If you're someone that is not very active, then watching your calories intake will be crucial to your success.

Reason being is that the less active you are, the less calories you are burning throughout the day. So you will have to make sure you watch what you eat compared to someone that is very active.

The faster your metabolism is, the more energy that will be burned allowing your to shed those pounds. So even if you have to take long walks during lunch breaks, or taking the stairs instead of the elevator, make sure you are burning those calories.

How does the Noom diet work?
Before you sign up, you have to answer some simple questions about your weight and how much you want to lose, and then the computer's algorithm will work out your weight loss goal and a weekly plan on how to achieve it.

"Essentially, Noom combines a calorie budget alongside information on which foods you should aim to eat more of, and which to eat less of," explains Dr Gall. "Noom's plans are non-restrictive, meaning that no foods are off limits, but it works to reinforce healthy eating habits by using a traffic light system."

The app even offers access to a "health coach" so you can ask direct questions (such as what to pick for dinner in a restaurant) when you're feeling stuck.

Benefits of Noom

Noom's program emphasizes a long-term approach to weight loss. It may have several benefits over quick-fix methods.

Focuses on calorie and nutrient density

Noom emphasizes calorie density, a measure of how many calories a food or beverage provides relative to its weight or volume. The program categorizes foods into a color system — green, yellow, and red — based on their calorie density and concentration of nutrients. Foods with the lowest calorie density, highest concentration of nutrients, or both, are considered green. Foods with the highest calorie density, lowest concentration of nutrients, or both, are labeled red, while yellow foods fall in between.

Calorie-dense foods contain a large number of calories in a small amount of food, whereas items of low calorie density have fewer calories in a large amount of food. Generally, low-calorie-dense foods, such as fruits and vegetables, contain more water and fiber and are low in fat.

On the other hand, high-calorie-dense foods, such as fatty fish, meats, nut butters, sweets, and desserts, typically provide fat or added sugars but lack water and fiber. Diets comprised mainly of low-calorie-dense foods and beverages are associated with less hunger, weight loss, and risk of chronic conditions like heart disease than diets rich in high-calorie-dense foods.

No food is off limits

Several popular diets can be restricting by limiting certain foods or entire food groups. This can promote disordered eating or obsessive behaviors surrounding healthy or "clean" eating. Noom takes the opposite approach, offering flexibility by allowing all foods to fit into your diet.

Because some high-calorie-dense foods like nuts contain important nutrients, and completely eliminating desserts and other treats is neither realistic nor worthwhile, Noom doesn't forbid these items but encourages less of them.

The program does this to help you stay within or near your daily calorie budget. Noom's library of recipes also helps you determine which foods and recipes are appropriate for you based on any food allergies or intolerances you may have.

Promotes behavioral changes

Losing weight and leading a healthy lifestyle goes beyond what and how much you eat. It's also about forming new healthy behaviors, reinforcing the healthy habits you already have, and breaking any unhealthy patterns that sabotage your goals.

Without behavioral change, any weight lost with a reduced-calorie diet tends to be regained over time — often in excess of what was initially lost. In fact, in a review of 29 long-term weight loss studies, people gained back 33% of their initial weight loss at 1 year, on average, and 79% after 5 years.

Recognizing that behavioral change is difficult, Noom uses a psychology-based curriculum that encourages self-efficacy — the belief in your ability to execute habits necessary to reach your goals.

In this way, Noom may better equip you with the tools and education necessary for effective behavioral change that underlies successful long-term weight loss maintenance. Indeed, one study found that 78% of nearly 36,000 Noom users sustained their weight loss over 9 months. It's unclear whether weight loss is sustained after this time.

What can you eat on the Noom diet?

"Foods classified as "green" foods are the ones that should make up the most of your diet, and have a low-calorie density, such as fruits, vegetables, fat-free dairy options and some grains," says Dr Gall.

Green foods include:

Spinach

Tomatoes

Carrots

Apples

Blueberries

Low-fat cheese

Almond milk

Tofu

Sweet potato

Peas

Brown rice

Bananas

"Yellow foods are ones that should be eaten moderately, such as lean meats and fish," says Dr Gall.

Yellow foods include:

Beans

Couscous

Olives

Avocado

Tuna

Houmous

Diet drinks

White bread

White rice

Guacamole

Salmon

"Red foods are the ones with a high-calorie density and the least nutritional value, so should only be eaten sparingly," says Dr Gall.

Red foods include:

Chips

Mayo

Juice

Cake

Chocolate

Beer

Nuts

Whole milk

Pizza

Hamburgers

Crisps

Why could the Noom diet work for you?

Seeing as most of us carry our phones everywhere, it's easy to track what you're eating – in fact, you'll probably only need to spend around 5-10 minutes a day on the app filling in your progress. Forgotten to add something in? Your health coach will prompt you to help you stay on track.

"Keeping a food diary can be incredibly helpful if you're trying to lose weight," says Dr Gall. "Being able to see what you're eating on a daily basis can help you to identify positive and negative eating habits, and can make you more aware of the calories that you consume. You may even be less likely to snack on foods with a high-calorie density as you'll know that you need to record it, so you might opt for healthier snacks instead."

And looking at the #NoomNerds hashtag on social media, results have been impressive, with a study claiming that out of 36,000 Noom users, 77.9 per cent reported weight loss.

Is there any evidence for its effectiveness?
Apps such as Noom encourage people to self-monitor their weight loss on a regular basis. One 2017 study found that people who frequently and consistently record their dietary habits experience more consistent and long-term weight loss.

However, self-monitoring weight loss is a practice that tends to decrease quickly over time. To prevent this, the Noom app provides features to motivate self-monitoring.

These features include access to a health coach and access to a social platform, where people can discuss their weight loss challenges and successes with other users.

Research into the Noom app

In 2016, some researchers conducted a study of the effectiveness of the Noom app. The study analyzed data from Noom users who recorded their diet at least twice per month for 6 months.

Of 35,921 Noom users, 77.9% reported a reduction in body weight while using the app. The researchers found that users who monitored their weight and dietary habits more frequently experienced more consistent weight loss.

A separate study, also from 2016, used Noom to deliver a diabetes prevention program (DPP) to 43 participants with prediabetes. At the start of the study, each participant had either overweight or obesity. The purpose of the study was to investigate the efficacy of the DPP in promoting weight loss among the participants.

The participants had experienced significant weight loss by week 16 and week 24 of using the DPP. Of the 36 participants who completed the study, 64% lost more than 5% of their body weight.

However, one limitation of the study is that it did not compare the Noom diet with any other app or diet. It is therefore difficult to know whether or not the Noom diet is more effective than other weight loss strategies.

Possible risks

A limitation of the Noom app is that it does not allow the user to record information on nutrients other than calories. However, a healthful diet should contain a good amount of micronutrients, such as vitamins and minerals.

As a result of this limitation, people using the Noom app will have limited information on the healthfulness of their food choices. It also means that doctors and dietitians may be reluctant to recommend the app.

Additionally, some Noom coaches do not have certification from the National Board for Health & Wellness Coaching. Coaches with this certification need to meet the minimum standard of knowledge and skills required for health and wellness coaching.

Coaches without this certification may offer inappropriate advice.

Also, people who have a complicated medical history should take extra care when using Noom and similar weight loss apps. These people should seek additional weight loss advice from a doctor, dietitian, or other healthcare professional.

Healthy recipes for some meals on a Noom Diet

Herbed Chicken Marsala

Ingredients

- Four 4-ounce boneless, skinless chicken breast cutlets
- Kosher salt and freshly ground black pepper
- 1/3 cup whole wheat flour
- 1 1/2 tablespoons extra-virgin olive oil
- 3/4 cup low-sodium chicken broth
- 1/3 cup sun-dried tomatoes (not packed in oil; not rehydrated), finely chopped or very thinly sliced
- 1/2 teaspoon finely chopped rosemary
- 10 ounces white button or cremini (baby bella) mushrooms, sliced
- 1/3 cup sweet marsala wine
- 2 teaspoons unsalted butter
- 1 to 2 tablespoons roughly chopped flat-leaf parsley

Directions

1. Place the chicken cutlets between 2 pieces of plastic wrap and pound with a meat mallet (or the flat side of a chef's knife) until about 1/3-inch thick. Sprinkle with 1/4 teaspoon salt and 1/4 teaspoon pepper.

2. Put the flour on a medium plate. Heat the oil in a large nonstick skillet over medium-high heat. Dredge the chicken in the flour to fully coat, shaking off any excess. Add the chicken to the skillet and fry until fully cooked and golden brown, about 4 minutes per side. Transfer to a platter and tent with foil to keep warm.

3. Add 1/2 cup of the broth, the sun-dried tomatoes and rosemary to any remaining drippings in the skillet and cook, stirring frequently, for 1 minute to plump the tomatoes. Add the mushrooms, 1/4 teaspoon salt and 1/2 teaspoon pepper and cook until the mushrooms are soft, about 5 minutes. Add the marsala and bring to a boil. Add the remaining 1/4 cup broth and the butter and simmer until the butter is fully melted, about 30 seconds.

4. Spoon the mushroom mixture and sauce over the chicken, sprinkle with the parsley and serve.

Cook's Note

This recipe uses regular whole wheat flour, but for a slightly more refined coating, whole wheat pastry flour can be substituted.

Lemony Yogurt Pound Cake
Ingredients

- Nonstick baking spray, for coating loaf pan
- 1 1/2 cups white whole wheat flour
- 2 teaspoons baking powder
- 1/4 teaspoon fine salt
- 3/4 cup sugar
- Finely grated zest of 1 lemon
- 1/2 cup plain lowfat (2-percent) Greek yogurt
- 1/4 cup lowfat (1-percent) milk
- 1/4 cup extra-virgin olive oil
- 1/2 teaspoon pure vanilla extract
- 2 large egg whites
- 1 large egg

Directions

1. Preheat the oven to 350 degrees F. Coat an 8 1/2- by 4 1/2-inch loaf pan with baking spray. Whisk together the flour, baking powder and salt in a medium bowl. Put the sugar and lemon zest in another bowl and rub the lemon zest into the sugar with your fingers.

2. Add the yogurt, milk, olive oil, vanilla, egg whites and whole egg and vigorously whisk until well blended. Add the flour mixture into the egg mixture and fold until just incorporated. Transfer to the prepared pan. Bake until a cake tester inserted in the center comes out clean, about 50 minutes. Cool in the pan on a wire rack for 5 minutes, and then unmold and cool to room temperature.

Sloppy Joes
Ingredients

- 1 pound extra-lean ground beef
- 1 onion, diced
- 4 cloves garlic, minced
- 1 jalapeno, minced
- 1 red pepper, diced
- 1 can small red beans or pinto beans, preferably low sodium drained and rinsed
- 1 1/2 cups no-salt-added tomato sauce

- 2 tablespoons tomato paste
- 1 tablespoon red wine vinegar
- 1 tablespoon molasses
- 1 tablespoon Worcestershire sauce
- 1 teaspoon mustard powder
- 3/4 teaspoon salt
- Freshly ground black pepper
- 8 whole-wheat burger buns

Directions

1. Brown the meat and the onion in a large nonstick skillet over medium-high heat for 5 minutes, breaking up the meat into crumbles as it cooks. Pour the drippings out of the pan and discard. Add the garlic, jalapeno, and red pepper and cook 5 minutes more, stirring occasionally. Stir in the rest of the ingredients, reduce heat to low, and simmer for 5 minutes more. Place a half-cup scoop of the mixture onto each bun and serve.

Pan-Seared Salmon with Kale and Apple Salad
Ingredients

- Four 5-ounce center-cut salmon fillets (about 1-inch thick)
- 3 tablespoons fresh lemon juice
- 3 tablespoons olive oil
- Kosher salt
- 1 bunch kale, ribs removed, leaves very thinly sliced (about 6 cups)
- 1/4 cup dates
- 1 Honeycrisp apple
- 1/4 cup finely grated pecorino
- 3 tablespoons toasted slivered almonds
- Freshly ground black pepper
- 4 whole wheat dinner rolls

Directions

1. Bring the salmon to room temperature 10 minutes before cooking.

2. Meanwhile, whisk together the lemon juice, 2 tablespoons of the olive oil and 1/4 teaspoon salt in a large bowl. Add the kale, toss to coat and let stand 10 minutes.

3. While the kale stands, cut the dates into thin slivers and the apple into matchsticks. Add the dates, apples, cheese and almonds to the kale. Season with pepper, toss well and set aside.

4. Sprinkle the salmon all over with 1/2 teaspoon salt and some pepper. Heat the remaining 1 tablespoon oil in a large nonstick skillet over medium-low heat. Raise the heat to medium-high. Place the salmon, skin-side up in the pan. Cook until golden brown on one side, about 4 minutes. Turn the fish over with a spatula, and cook until it feels firm to the touch, about 3 minutes more.

5. Divide the salmon, salad and rolls evenly among four plates.

Lentil Vegetable Soup
Ingredients

- 1 pound French green lentils

- 4 cups chopped yellow onions (3 large onions)

- 4 cups chopped leeks, white part only (2 leeks)

- 1 tablespoon minced garlic (3 cloves)

- 1/4 cup good olive oil, plus additional for drizzling on top

- 1 tablespoon kosher salt

- 1 1/2 teaspoons freshly ground black pepper
- 1 tablespoon minced fresh thyme leaves or 1 teaspoon dried
- 1 teaspoon ground cumin
- 3 cups medium-diced celery (8 stalks)
- 3 cups medium-diced carrots (4 to 6 carrots)
- 3 quarts chicken stock
- 1/4 cup tomato paste
- 2 tablespoons red wine or red wine vinegar
- Freshly grated Parmesan cheese

Directions

1. In a large bowl, cover the lentils with boiling water and allow to sit for 15 minutes. Drain.

2. In a large stockpot on medium heat, saute the onions, leeks, and garlic with the olive oil, salt, pepper, thyme, and cumin for 20 minutes, until the vegetables are translucent and very tender. Add the celery and carrots and saute for 10 more minutes. Add the chicken stock, tomato paste, and lentils. Cover and bring to a boil. Reduce the heat and simmer uncovered for 1 hour, until the lentils are cooked through. Check the seasonings.

Add the red wine and serve hot, drizzled with olive oil and sprinkled with grated Parmesan.

Mixed Berries and Banana Smoothie
Ingredients

Smoothie:

- 1 cup frozen mixed berries
- 3/4 cup orange juice
- 1/4 cup low-fat vanilla yogurt
- 1 frozen ripe banana
- 1 teaspoon honey, optional

Toppings for a Smoothie Bowl:

- 1/4 cup fresh blueberries
- 1/4 cup fresh raspberries
- 2 dollops low-fat vanilla yogurt
- 2 to 3 tablespoons granola
- 1 teaspoon chia seeds

Directions

1. For the smoothie: Combine the berries, orange juice, yogurt, banana and honey, if using, in a blender and puree until smooth.

2. For the toppings: Pour the smoothie into a bowl. Top with the blueberries, raspberries, vanilla yogurt and granola. Sprinkle with the chia seeds.

Breakfast Casserole

Ingredients

- 8 ounces spicy or sweet turkey sausage links, casings removed, meat crumbled

- 2 scallions, sliced

- 6 large eggs and 6 large egg whites

- 1 3/4 cups 1-percent milk

- Kosher salt and freshly ground black pepper

- One 9-ounce package frozen chopped spinach, thawed and drained of excess liquid

- 3/4 cup shredded Cheddar

- 1/2 cup grated Parmesan

- 1/2 whole wheat baguette, cut into 3/4-inch cubes (about 4 cups)

- Cooking spray

Directions

1. Heat a large nonstick skillet over medium heat. Add the turkey and scallions and cook, stirring to break up any large chunks, until browned and cooked through, about 10 minutes. Remove from heat and let cool slightly.

2. Whisk the eggs, egg whites, milk and 1/2 teaspoon each salt and pepper in a large bowl until combined. Add the cooked sausage, spinach, cheeses and bread and toss to distribute ingredients evenly.

3. Spray a 3-quart casserole dish with cooking spray. Spread the egg mixture evenly in the dish. Cover and refrigerate for at least 6 hours or preferably overnight.

4. Preheat the oven to 350 degrees F. Bake the casserole, uncovered, until set and lightly browned on top, about 30 minutes.

Cook's Note

Make-Ahead Tip: Freeze the baked casserole for up to 2 weeks. Cover with foil and reheat at 350 degrees F until hot, 35 to 45 minutes.

Broiled Salmon with Herb Mustard Glaze
Ingredients

- 2 garlic cloves
- 3/4 teaspoon finely chopped fresh rosemary leaves
- 3/4 teaspoon finely chopped fresh thyme leaves
- 1 tablespoon dry white wine
- 1 tablespoon extra-virgin olive oil
- 2 tablespoons Dijon mustard
- 2 tablespoons whole-grain mustard
- Nonstick olive oil cooking spray
- Six 6- to 8-ounce salmon fillets
- Salt and freshly ground black pepper
- 6 lemon wedges

Directions

1. In a mini food processor, combine garlic, rosemary, thyme, wine, oil, Dijon mustard, and 1 tablespoon of whole-grain mustard. Grind the mustard sauce until combined, about 30 seconds. Transfer to a small bowl. Add remaining 1 tablespoon of whole-grain mustard to the sauce and stir to combine. Set aside mustard sauce.

2. Preheat the broiler. Line a heavy rimmed baking sheet with foil. Spray the foil with nonstick spray. Arrange the

salmon fillets on the baking sheet and sprinkle them with salt and pepper. Broil for 2 minutes. Spoon the mustard sauce over the fillets. Continue broiling until the fillets are just cooked through and golden brown, about 5 minutes longer.

3. Transfer the fillets to plates and serve with lemon wedges.

Whole30 Bacon and Egg Cups
Ingredients

- 12 strips sugar-free bacon (about 10 ounces)

- 2 red potatoes, sliced 1/8 inch thick, rounded ends discarded

- 1 small red bell pepper, finely chopped

- 12 large eggs

- 2 tablespoons chopped fresh chives

- Hot sauce, for serving

Directions

1. Preheat the oven to 400 degrees F. Wrap 1 piece of bacon around the inside of each cup of a 12-cup muffin tin to create rings. Put 1 slice of potato on the bottom of

each cup and divide the bell pepper pieces among the cups.

2. Bake until the fat starts to render from the bacon (it will bubble in the bottom of each cup) and the bacon begins to crisp and turn light brown on the top edges, 10 to 12 minutes.

3. Remove the tin from the oven and crack an egg into each cup, making sure the yolk is inside the bacon ring. Continue baking until the bacon is crisp, the egg whites are cooked through and the yolks are still runny, about 10 minutes longer. Run an offset spatula around the edges and remove to a platter. Sprinkle with the chives and serve with hot sauce if desired.

Slow-Cooker Pork Tacos
Ingredients

- 3 whole ancho chiles
- 3 whole pasilla chiles
- 4 cloves garlic, unpeeled
- 2 to 3 chipotles in adobo sauce
- 1/2 medium white onion, roughly chopped
- 3 tablespoons extra-virgin olive oil
- 2 tablespoons honey

- 1 tablespoon cider vinegar
- Kosher salt
- 2 teaspoons dried oregano, preferably Mexican
- 3 3/4 cups low-sodium chicken broth
- 4 pounds boneless pork shoulder (untrimmed), cut into chunks
- Freshly ground pepper
- 2 bay leaves
- 1 cinnamon stick
- Corn tortillas, warmed, for serving
- Assorted taco toppings, for garnish

Directions

1. Put the ancho and pasilla chiles and the garlic in a bowl; add 2 to 3 tablespoons water. Microwave on high until soft and pliable, 2 to 3 minutes. Stem and seed the chiles; peel the garlic. Transfer the chiles and garlic to a blender.

2. Add the chipotles, onion, 2 tablespoons olive oil, honey, vinegar, 1 tablespoon salt and the oregano to the blender; puree until smooth. Heat the remaining 1 tablespoon oil in a large skillet over high heat; add the

chile sauce and fry, stirring, until thick and fragrant, about 8 minutes. Pour in the broth and reduce until slightly thickened.

3. Season the pork all over with salt and pepper and transfer to a large slow cooker. Add the bay leaves and cinnamon stick, then pour in the sauce. Cover and cook on high until the meat is tender, about 5 hours. (Or cook the meat in a large Dutch oven, covered, for 1 hour 45 minutes at 350 degrees; uncover and cook 30 more minutes.)

4. Discard the bay leaves and cinnamon stick. Shred the pork with 2 forks; season with salt and pepper. Serve the shredded pork in the tortillas, along with toppings.

Vegetable Noodle Soup
Ingredients

- 2 tablespoons extra-virgin olive oil

- 1 rib celery, sliced (about 1 cup)

- 1 medium carrot, sliced (about 3/4 cup)

- 1 clove garlic, smashed

- 1/4 medium onion, about 1/2 cup

- 1/4 teaspoon kosher salt

- 1/3 cup orzo or other small pasta or egg noodles or broken up spaghetti
- 4 cups low-sodium chicken broth (1-quart box, or 2 cans)
- Small handful fresh parsley leaves, basil or dill, chopped (about 2 tablespoons)
- 1/2 lemon, juiced (about 1 tablespoon)
- Freshly ground black pepper
- Serving suggestion: Whole-wheat crackers and cheese sticks.

Directions

1. Heat the olive oil in a medium saucepan over medium heat; add all the vegetables, garlic and onion. Season with the salt, and cook until tender, about 6 minutes. Add the pasta and cook until slightly toasted and golden, about 2 minutes. Add broth, and bring to a boil over high heat. Cook, covered, until pasta is just tender, about 8 minutes.

2. Stir in whatever herb suits you (or your young eater) and lemon juice. Season with pepper and additional salt, to taste. Fill thermos, pack in a lunch sack with crackers and cheese sticks and send off to school.

Cook's Note

This soup freezes well, so freeze any leftovers or make a double batch to have plenty on hand. Also, you can stir in some cooked chicken or mini-meatballs, if desired, for another meal.

Angel Food Cake
Ingredients

- 1 3/4 cups sugar
- 1/4 teaspoon salt
- 1 cup cake flour, sifted
- 12 egg whites (the closer to room temperature the better)
- 1/3 cup warm water
- 1 teaspoon orange extract, or extract of your choice
- 1 1/2 teaspoons cream of tartar

Directions

1. Preheat oven to 350 degrees F.

2. In a food processor spin sugar about 2 minutes until it is superfine. Sift half of the sugar with the salt the cake flour, setting the remaining sugar aside.

3. In a large bowl, use a balloon whisk to thoroughly combine egg whites, water, orange extract, and cream of tartar. After 2 minutes, switch to a hand mixer. Slowly sift the reserved sugar, beating continuously at medium speed. Once you have achieved medium peaks, sift enough of the flour mixture in to dust the top of the foam. Using a spatula fold in gently. Continue until all of the flour mixture is incorporated.

4. Carefully spoon mixture into an ungreased tube pan. Bake for 35 minutes before checking for doneness with a wooden skewer. (When inserted halfway between the inner and outer wall, the skewer should come out dry).

5. Cool upside down on cooling rack for at least an hour before removing from pan.

Cook's Note

Since they're easier to separate use the freshest eggs you can get.

Blueberry Compote
Ingredients

- 2 cups frozen blueberries
- 3 tablespoons water
- 1/4 cup sugar
- 2 teaspoons lemon juice

Directions

1. Combine 1 cup of the blueberries, water, sugar and lemon juice in a small saucepan. Cook over a medium heat for about 10 minutes. Add the rest of the blueberries and cook for 8 minutes more, stirring frequently. Serve warm.

Chicken Saltimbocca
Ingredients

- 6 (3-ounce) chicken cutlets, pounded to evenly flatten
- Salt and freshly ground black pepper
- 6 paper-thin slices prosciutto
- 1 (10-ounce) box frozen chopped spinach, thawed
- 3 tablespoons olive oil
- 1/4 cup grated Parmesan
- 1 (14-ounce) can low-salt chicken broth

- 2 tablespoons fresh lemon juice

Directions

1. Place the chicken cutlets flat on the work surface. Sprinkle the chicken with salt and pepper. Lay 1 slice of prosciutto atop each chicken cutlet.

2. Squeeze the frozen spinach to remove the excess water. Season the spinach with salt and pepper. In a small bowl, toss the spinach with 1 tablespoon of oil to coat.

3. Arrange an even, thin layer of spinach atop the prosciutto slices. Sprinkle the Parmesan evenly over each. Beginning at the short tapered end, roll up each chicken cutlet as for a jellyroll. Secure with a toothpick.

4. Heat the remaining 2 tablespoons of oil in a heavy large skillet over high heat. Add the chicken and cook just until golden brown, about 2 minutes per side. Add the chicken broth and lemon juice, and scrape the browned bits off the bottom of the pan with a wooden spoon. Bring the liquid to a boil. Reduce the heat to medium. Cover and simmer until the chicken is just cooked through, about 8 to 10 minutes. Transfer the chicken to a platter. Simmer the cooking liquid over high heat until it is reduced to about 2/3 cup, about 5 minutes. Season the cooking liquid with salt and pepper, to taste. Remove

toothpicks from the chicken. Drizzle the reduced cooking liquid over the chicken and serve immediately.

Spaghetti Squash and Meatballs
Ingredients

- 1 medium spaghetti squash (about 2 pounds)
- Kosher salt
- 3 tablespoons extra-virgin olive oil, plus more for brushing
- 2 stalks celery, chopped
- 1 medium carrot, roughly chopped
- 1 medium onion, roughly chopped
- 6 cloves garlic
- 1 cup fresh parsley leaves
- 1 pound ground beef
- 1 pound ground pork
- 2 large eggs
- 1 cup Italian-style breadcrumbs
- 1 cup plus 3 tablespoons grated parmesan cheese
- 2 28-ounce cans tomato puree

- 2 large sprigs basil
- 1 teaspoon dried oregano

Directions

1. Preheat the oven to 425 degrees F. Halve the squash lengthwise and scoop out the seeds. Sprinkle the cut sides with 1/2 teaspoon salt, then brush both sides with olive oil. Put the squash, cut-side up, in a baking dish and cover tightly with aluminum foil. Roast 20 minutes, then uncover and continue roasting until the squash is tender, about 35 more minutes.

2. Meanwhile, make the meatballs: Brush a baking sheet with olive oil. Pulse the celery, carrot, onion, garlic and parsley in a food processor to make a paste. Transfer half of the vegetable paste to a bowl; add the ground beef, ground pork, eggs, breadcrumbs, 1 cup parmesan and 1 teaspoon salt and mix with your hands until just combined. Form into about 24 two-inch meatballs; transfer to the prepared baking sheet. Bake until firm but not cooked through, about 10 minutes.

3. Make the sauce: Heat 3 tablespoons olive oil in a large pot over medium-high heat. Add the remaining vegetable paste and cook, stirring occasionally, until it looks dry, about 5 minutes. Stir in the tomato puree; rinse each can with 1 cup water and add to the pot. Stir

in the basil, oregano and 1 1/2 teaspoons salt. Bring to a simmer, then add the meatballs and simmer until the sauce thickens and the meatballs are cooked through, 15 to 20 minutes. Remove the basil.

4. Use a fork to scrape the spaghetti squash flesh into strands; transfer to a large bowl and toss with 2 tablespoons grated parmesan. Season with salt. Divide the squash among bowls and top each with some meatballs, sauce and the remaining 1 tablespoon parmesan.

5. This recipe makes extra sauce and meatballs. Let cool completely, then freeze in a storage container for up to one month.

Buffalo Cauliflower with Blue Cheese Sauce
Ingredients

Cheese Sauce:

- 1/3 cup nonfat sour cream
- 2 tablespoons crumbled blue cheese
- 1 tablespoon skim milk
- 2 teaspoons mayonnaise
- Kosher salt and freshly ground black pepper

Buffalo Cauliflower:

- 2 tablespoons unsalted butter
- 1/4 cup hot sauce, such as Frank's
- 1 tablespoon freshly squeezed lemon juice
- 2 tablespoons olive oil
- Kosher salt
- 8 cups cauliflower florets (from about 1 medium head)

Directions

1. Preheat the oven to 400 degrees F.

2. For the cheese sauce: Whisk together the sour cream, blue cheese, milk, mayonnaise, 1/8 teaspoon salt and a few grinds of pepper in a small bowl. Cover and refrigerate until chilled, about 30 minutes

3. For the Buffalo cauliflower: Meanwhile, microwave the butter in a small microwave-safe bowl on high until melted. Whisk in the hot sauce and lemon juice and set aside.

4. Mix olive oil, 1/4 teaspoon salt and 1/2 cup water in a large bowl. Add the cauliflower and toss until well coated. Spread the cauliflower on a rimmed baking sheet and roast until beginning to brown and just tender, 20 to

25 minutes. Whisk the hot sauce mixture again, drizzle over the cauliflower and toss with tongs to coat. Roast the cauliflower until the sauce is bubbling and browned around the edges, 5 to 7 minutes more. Serve hot with the cheese sauce.

Roasted Cauliflower and Broccoli

Ingredients

- 1 small head cauliflower (2 pounds), cut into florets
- 2 large stalks broccoli (1 pound), cut into florets
- 1 head garlic, broken into cloves
- 2 tablespoons olive oil
- 1/2 teaspoon salt

Directions

1. Preheat the oven to 375 degrees F.

2. Place cauliflower and broccoli into a 9 by 13 inch baking dish, toss with the olive oil, and sprinkle with salt. Cover the dish and bake for 1/2 hour. Remove the cover, stir and cook for 30 to 40 minutes more, until vegetables are tender and nicely browned, stirring occasionally.

Tuscan Vegetable Soup
Ingredients

- 1 (15-ounce) can low-sodium canellini beans, drained and rinsed
- 1 tablespoon olive oil
- 1/2 large onion, diced (about 1 cup)
- 2 carrots, diced (about 1/2 cup)
- 2 stalks celery, diced, (about 1/2 cup)
- 1 small zucchini, diced (about 1 1/2 cups)
- 1 clove garlic, minced
- 1 tablespoon chopped fresh thyme leaves (or 1 teaspoon dried)
- 2 teaspoons chopped fresh sage leaves (or 1/2 teaspoon dried)
- 1/2 teaspoon salt
- 1/4 teaspoon freshly ground black pepper
- 32 ounces low-sodium chicken broth or vegetable broth
- 1 (14.5-ounce) can no salt added diced tomatoes
- 2 cups chopped baby spinach leaves
- 1/3 cup freshly grated Parmesan, optional

Directions

1. In a small bowl mash half of the beans with a masher or the back of a spoon, and set aside.

2. Heat the oil in a large soup pot over medium-high heat. Add the onion, carrots, celery, zucchini, garlic, thyme, sage, 1/2 teaspoon of salt and 1/4 teaspoon of pepper, and cook stirring occasionally until the vegetables are tender, about 5 minutes.

3. Add the broth and tomatoes with the juice and bring to a boil. Add the mashed and whole beans and the spinach leaves and cook until the spinach is wilted, about 3 minutes more.

4. Serve topped with Parmesan, if desired.

Three Bean and Beef Chili
Ingredients

- 1 tablespoon olive oil
- 1 onion, diced (1 cup)
- 1 red bell pepper, diced (1 cup)
- 2 carrots, diced (1/2 cup)
- 2 teaspoons ground cumin
- 1 pound extra-lean ground beef (90 percent lean)

- One 28-ounce can crushed tomatoes
- 2 cups water
- 1 chipotle chile in adobo sauce, seeded and minced
- 2 teaspoons adobo sauce from the can of chipotles
- 1/2 teaspoon dried oregano
- Salt and freshly ground black pepper
- One 15.5-ounce can black beans, drained and rinsed
- One 15.5-ounce can kidney beans, drained and rinsed
- One 15.5-ounce can pinto beans, drained and rinsed

Directions

1. Heat the oil in large pot or Dutch oven over moderate heat. Add the onion, bell pepper and carrots, cover and cook, stirring occasionally until the vegetables are soft, about 10 minutes. Add the cumin and cook, stirring, for 1 minute. Add the ground beef; raise the heat to high and cook, breaking up the meat with a spoon, until the meat is no longer pink. Stir in the tomatoes, water, chipotle and adobo sauce, oregano and salt and pepper. Simmer, partially covered, stirring from time to time, for 30 minutes. Stir in the beans and cook, partially covered, 20 minutes longer. Season, to taste, with salt and pepper.

Lemon-Garlic Shrimp and Grits

Ingredients

- 3/4 cup instant grits
- Kosher salt and freshly ground black pepper
- 1/4 cup grated parmesan cheese
- 3 tablespoons unsalted butter
- 1 1/4 pounds medium shrimp, peeled and deveined (tails intact)
- 2 large cloves garlic, minced
- Pinch of cayenne pepper (optional)
- Juice of 1/2 lemon, plus wedges for serving
- 2 tablespoons roughly chopped fresh parsley

Directions

1. Bring 3 cups water to a boil in a medium saucepan over high heat, covered. Uncover and slowly whisk in the grits, 1 teaspoon salt and 1/2 teaspoon black pepper. Reduce the heat to medium low and cook, stirring occasionally, until thickened, about 5 minutes. Stir in the parmesan and 1 tablespoon butter. Remove from the heat and season with salt and black pepper. Cover to keep warm.

2. Meanwhile, season the shrimp with salt and black pepper. Melt the remaining 2 tablespoons butter in a large skillet over medium-high heat. Add the shrimp, garlic and cayenne, if using, and cook, tossing, until the shrimp are pink, 3 to 4 minutes. Remove from the heat and add 2 tablespoons water, the lemon juice and parsley; stir to coat the shrimp with the sauce and season with salt and black pepper.

3. Divide the grits among shallow bowls and top with the shrimp and sauce. Serve with lemon wedges.

Oil and Vinegar Slaw
Ingredients

- 1/4 cup red wine vinegar
- 2 tablespoons sugar
- 2 tablespoons peanut or vegetable oil, eyeball it
- 1 sack, 16 ounces, shredded cabbage mix for slaw salads
- 1 teaspoon salt
- Salt and pepper

Directions

1. Mix vinegar and sugar. Add oil. Add cabbage to dressing and season with salt and pepper. Toss with fingers to combine. Adjust seasoning. Let stand 20 minutes. Re-toss and serve.

Quinoa Salad
Ingredients

- 12 cups water
- 1 1/2 cups quinoa, rinsed
- 5 pickling cucumbers, peeled, ends trimmed, and cut into 1/4-inch cubes
- 1 small red onion, cut into 1/4-inch cubes
- 1 large tomato, cored, seeded, and diced
- 1 bunch Italian parsley leaves, chopped
- 2 bunches mint leaves, chopped
- 1/2 cup extra-virgin olive oil
- 1/4 cup red wine vinegar
- 1 lemon, juiced
- 1 1/2 teaspoons salt
- 3/4 teaspoon freshly ground black pepper

- 4 heads endive, trimmed and separated into individual spears
- 1 avocado, peeled, seeded and diced, for garnish

Directions

1. Bring the water to a boil in a large saucepan. Add the quinoa, stir once, and return to a boil. Cook uncovered, over medium heat for 12 minutes. Strain and rinse well with cold water, shaking the sieve well to remove all moisture.

2. When dry, transfer the quinoa to a large bowl. Add the cucumbers, onion, tomato, parsley, mint, olive oil, vinegar, lemon juice, salt, and pepper and toss well. Spoon onto endive spears, top with avocado, and serve.

Teriyaki Chicken Thighs
Ingredients

- 1/4 cup low-sodium soy sauce
- 2 tablespoons brown sugar
- 2 tablespoons dry sherry
- 2 tablespoons rice vinegar
- 2 garlic cloves, crushed with a garlic press or minced

- 1 teaspoon finely grated fresh ginger
- 1/4 teaspoon red pepper flakes
- 2 pounds skinless chicken thighs
- 2 teaspoons sesame seeds

Directions

1. Combine the soy sauce, sugar, sherry, vinegar, garlic, ginger and red pepper flakes and stir until the sugar dissolves. Transfer to a resealable plastic bag and add the chicken. Seal the bag and marinate the chicken in the refrigerator, turning once, for 1 hour. The chicken can be marinated for up to 4 hours.

2. Heat the broiler to high. Arrange the chicken on a broiler pan skin side down and broil until brown and crispy, 8 to 10 minutes. Flip the chicken and broil until almost cooked through, about 8 minutes longer. Sprinkle with sesame seeds and cook until the seeds turn golden brown and the chicken is done, 1 to 2 minutes longer.

Shrimp Stir-Fry
Ingredients

- 1 tablespoon butter
- 1 tablespoon olive oil

- 2 pounds jumbo shrimp, peeled and deveined, tails on
- 4 cloves garlic, minced
- 2 large zucchini, diced
- 2 large ears of corn, kernels removed
- 3/4 cup red grape tomatoes, sliced in half lengthwise
- 3/4 cup yellow grape tomatoes, sliced in half lengthwise
- Salt and freshly ground black pepper
- 12 to 18 fresh basil leaves, cut in chiffonade
- Parmesan shavings
- Juice of 1 lemon
- Rice or pasta, for serving, optional

Directions

1. Melt the butter with the olive oil in a large skillet over a medium-high heat. Add the shrimp and garlic, then saute until the shrimp are opaque, about 3 minutes. Remove the shrimp to a plate.

2. Increase the heat to high, then throw in the zucchini. Stir it around for about 45 seconds, then scoot the zucchini to the edges of the pan. Throw in the corn and

cook it for a minute, then push it to the edges of the pan. Throw in the grape tomatoes, stir them around for a minute, then sprinkle on some salt and pepper to taste.

3. Then throw the shrimp back in. Stir everything around for about 45 seconds, or until it's all combined and hot. Then pour it onto a big platter.

4. Sprinkle on the fresh basil and some Parmesan shavings then ... this is the best part ... squeeze the lemon all over the top. This adds a wonderful, indescribable freshness.

5. You can serve this with rice, with pasta or it's just perfect on its own.

Low-Cal Fettuccine Alfredo
Ingredients

- 1 tablespoon unsalted butter
- 1 clove garlic, minced
- 1 teaspoon grated lemon zest
- 2 teaspoons all-purpose flour
- 1 cup low-fat (2%) milk
- Kosher salt
- 2 tablespoons Neufchtel or low-fat cream cheese

- 3/4 cup grated parmesan cheese, plus more for topping
- 3 tablespoons chopped fresh parsley
- 12 ounces fresh fettuccine
- Freshly ground pepper

Directions

1. Make the sauce: Melt the butter in a skillet over medium heat. Add the garlic and lemon zest and cook until the garlic is slightly soft, about 1 minute. Add in the flour and cook, stirring with a wooden spoon, 1 minute. Whisk in the milk and 3/4 teaspoon salt and cook, whisking constantly, until just thickened, about 3 minutes. Add the Neufchatel and parmesan cheese; whisk until melted, about 1 minute. Stir in the chopped parsley.

2. Meanwhile, bring a large pot of salted water to a boil. Add the fettuccine and cook until al dente, 2 to 3 minutes. Reserve 1 cup cooking water, then drain the pasta and return to the pot. Add the sauce and 1/2 cup of the reserved cooking water to the pasta and gently toss to combine, adding more cooking water as needed to loosen. Season with salt. Divide among bowls and top with parmesan and pepper.

Marinated Chicken Breasts

Ingredients

- 1 to 2 tablespoons vinegar, like cider, balsamic, or red wine
- 2 to 3 teaspoons dried herbs, like thyme, oregano, rosemary, or crumbled bay leaf
- 1 to 2 tablespoons mustard, whole grain or Dijon
- 1 to 2 teaspoon garlic or onion powder, optional
- 1/4 cup extra-virgin olive oil
- Kosher salt and freshly ground black pepper
- 4 boneless, skinless chicken breast, each about 6 ounces

Directions

1. Put the vinegar, herbs, mustard, powders if using and oil in a large re-sealable plastic bag. Close the bag and shake to combine all the ingredients. Open the bag, drop in the chicken breast in the bag. Close and shake the bag to coat evenly. Freeze for up to 2 weeks.

2. Thaw in the refrigerator overnight, under cold, running water, or in the microwave at 30 percent power for 1 minute at a time.

3. Heat a grill or grill pan. When the grill is hot, place the chicken on the grill and cook for about 4 minutes per side, or until cooked through. You can also bake the thawed chicken in a 375 degree F oven for 15 minutes, or until cooked through.

Breakfast Burrito
Ingredients

- 2 teaspoons canola oil
- 1/2 small red onion, diced (1 cup)
- 1 red bell pepper, seeded and diced
- 1 cup drained, rinsed canned black beans, preferably low-sodium
- 1/4 teaspoon chili flakes
- Salt and freshly ground black pepper
- 4 eggs and 4 egg whites
- 1/3 cup (about 1 1/2 ounce) shredded pepper Jack cheese
- Nonstick cooking spray
- 4 (10 inch) whole wheat tortillas (burrito size)
- 1/4 cup reduced fat-free sour cream or 2 percent plain Greek yogurt

- 1/4 cup salsa
- 1 large tomato, (4 ounces) seeded and diced
- 1 small avocado (4 ounces), cubed
- Hot sauce

Directions

1. Heat the canola oil in a large nonstick skillet over a medium-high heat. Cook the onions and peppers until onions are softened and peppers are slightly charred, about 8 minutes. Add black beans and red pepper flakes and cook until warmed through, another 3 minutes. Season with salt and pepper and transfer to a dish.

2. Whisk together the eggs and egg whites then stir in the cheese. Spray the skillet with cooking spray, and reheat the skillet over a medium heat. Reduce heat to low and add eggs, scrambling until cooked through, about 3 minutes. Spread each tortilla with 1 tablespoon each sour cream (or yogurt) and salsa, then layer with 1/4 of the black bean mixture, 1/4 of the scrambled eggs, some diced tomato and 1/4 of the avocado. Season, to taste, with hot sauce. Roll up burrito-style and serve.

Chia Seed Pudding
Ingredients

- 1 cup vanilla-flavored unsweetened almond milk
- 1 cup plain low-fat (2 percent) Greek yogurt
- 2 tablespoons pure maple syrup (preferably grade B), plus 4 teaspoons for serving
- 1 teaspoon pure vanilla extract
- Kosher salt
- 1/4 cup chia seeds
- 1 pint strawberries, hulled and chopped
- 1/4 cup sliced almonds, toasted

Directions

1. In a medium bowl, gently whisk the almond milk, yogurt, 2 tablespoons maple syrup, the vanilla and 1/8 teaspoon salt until just blended. Whisk in the chia seeds; let stand 30 minutes. Stir to distribute the seeds if they have settled. Cover and refrigerate overnight.

2. The next day, in a medium bowl, toss the berries with the remaining 4 teaspoons maple syrup. Mix in the almonds.

3. Spoon the pudding into 4 bowls or glasses; mound the berry mixture on top and serve.

Healthified Broccoli Cheddar Soup

Ingredients

- 1 bunch broccoli
- 1 small onion, finely chopped
- 1 medium red-skinned potato, diced
- 1/4 cup all-purpose flour
- 3 cups low-sodium chicken or vegetable broth
- Kosher salt and freshly ground black pepper
- 1/4 teaspoon freshly grated nutmeg
- 1 cup grated extra-sharp Cheddar
- 1 teaspoon Worcestershire sauce
- One 12-ounce can fat-free evaporated milk
- 2 scallions, thinly sliced

Directions

1. Separate the stems and the florets from the broccoli. Trim and discard the bottom of the broccoli stems and peel the tough outer layers. Finely chop the stems and coarsely chop the florets and set aside separately.

2. Mist a large pot with nonstick cooking spray and heat over medium heat. Add the broccoli stems, onions and

potatoes and cook, stirring, until softened, 7 to 10 minutes. Add the flour and cook, stirring, until lightly toasted, about 2 minutes. Stir in the broth and bring to a boil. Reduce the heat to maintain a simmer and continue to cook, stirring occasionally, until thickened and the vegetables are tender, 12 to 15 minutes.

3. Meanwhile, combine the reserved florets and 1/2 cup water in a small saucepan. Bring to a boil, cover and continue to steam until the florets are bright green and crisp-tender, about 5 minutes. Add the entire contents of the pot with the florets to the soup along with the nutmeg. Stir to combine and remove from the heat. Stir in the Cheddar, Worcestershire and milk. Season with salt and pepper. Garnish with the scallions.

Cook's Note

Leftover soup should be reheated in the microwave rather than the stovetop, where the cheese will "break" or separate from the broth.

Pork Chops With Apples and Garlic Smashed Potatoes
Ingredients

- 1 pound small fingerling potatoes
- 2 cloves garlic

- Kosher salt
- 4 1/2-inch-thick boneless pork loin chops (5 ounces each)
- 2 teaspoons chopped fresh sage
- Freshly ground pepper
- 1 tablespoon extra-virgin olive oil
- 1 large red onion, cut into 1/2-inch wedges
- 2 Granny Smith apples, cut into 1/2-inch pieces
- 3/4 cup apple cider
- 1/4 cup buttermilk

Directions

1. Put the potatoes and garlic in a saucepan, cover with cold water and season with salt. Cover and bring to a boil, then uncover and continue cooking until tender, about 15 minutes. Cover and set aside.

2. Meanwhile, rub both sides of the pork chops with the sage, and salt and pepper to taste. Heat a large cast-iron skillet over high heat, then add 1 teaspoon olive oil and sear the chops until golden on both sides, about 5 minutes total. Transfer to a plate. Wipe out the skillet and add the remaining 2 teaspoons olive oil. Add the

onion and apples and cook over medium-high heat until lightly browned, about 5 minutes. Season with salt and pepper and stir in the cider.

3. Return the chops to the skillet. Cover and cook, turning once, until just cooked through, 4 to 5 minutes. Drain the potatoes, reserving 1/4 cup liquid. Return the potatoes to the pan; add the buttermilk and mash, adding cooking liquid as needed. Season with salt and pepper. Serve with the pork chops, onion and apples. Drizzle with the pan juices.

Hasselback Sweet Potatoes
Ingredients

- 4 medium sweet potatoes

- 1 tablespoon unsalted butter, melted

- 1 teaspoon olive oil

- 1 teaspoon finely chopped fresh thyme leaves

- 1 garlic clove, finely grated on a microplane

- Kosher salt and freshly ground black pepper

- 1/3 cup nonfat Greek-style yogurt

- 1 scallion, white and green parts chopped

Directions

1. Preheat the oven to 425 degrees F. Line a baking sheet with aluminum foil.

2. Make a series of 1/8-inch slices along each potato, slicing 2/3 of the way through.

3. Stir together the butter, oil, thyme, garlic, 1/4 teaspoon salt and 1/4 teaspoon pepper in a small bowl. Rub the potatoes all over with the mixture, getting in between the slices.

4. Place on the baking sheet and roast until the center of the potatoes are tender and the outside is crisp, 50 minutes to 1 hour. Halfway through the roasting time, remove the potatoes from the oven and run a fork gently across the tops of the potatoes, using light pressure, to fan the slices and separate them from one another.

5. Meanwhile, stir the yogurt and scallions with a pinch salt and a pinch pepper. Serve the sauce with the potatoes.

Herb-Marinated Pork Tenderloins
Ingredients

- 1 lemon, zest grated
- 3/4 cup freshly squeezed lemon juice (4 to 6 lemons)

- Good olive oil
- 2 tablespoons minced garlic (6 cloves)
- 1 1/2 tablespoons minced fresh rosemary leaves
- 1 tablespoon chopped fresh thyme leaves
- 2 teaspoons Dijon mustard
- Kosher salt
- 3 pork tenderloins (about 1 pound each)
- Freshly ground black pepper

Directions

1. Combine the lemon zest, lemon juice, 1/2 cup olive oil, garlic, rosemary, thyme, mustard, and 2 teaspoons salt in a sturdy 1-gallon resealable plastic bag. Add the pork tenderloins and turn to coat with the marinade. Squeeze out the air and seal the bag. Marinate the pork in the refrigerator for at least 3 hours but preferably overnight.

2. Preheat the oven to 400 degrees F.

3. Remove the tenderloins from the marinade and discard the marinade but leave the herbs that cling to the meat. Sprinkle the tenderloins generously with salt and pepper. Heat 3 tablespoons olive oil in a large oven-proof saute pan over medium-high heat. Sear the pork

tenderloins on all sides until golden brown. Place the saute pan in the oven and roast the tenderloins for 10 to 15 minutes or until the meat registers 137 degrees F at the thickest part. Transfer the tenderloins to a platter and cover tightly with aluminum foil. Allow to rest for 10 minutes. Carve in 1/2-inch-thick diagonal slices. The thickest part of the tenderloin will be quite pink (it's just fine!) and the thinnest part will be well done. Season with salt and pepper and serve warm, or at room temperature with the juices that collect in the platter.

Pasta and Beans: Pasta e Fagioli
Ingredients

- 2 tablespoons (2 turns around the pan) extra-virgin olive oil

- 1/8 pound (about 3 slices) pancetta, chopped

- Two 4 to 6-inch sprigs rosemary, left intact

- One 4 to 6-inch sprig thyme with several sprigs on it, left intact

- 1 large fresh bay leaf or 2 dried bay leaves

- 1 medium onion, finely chopped

- 1 small carrot, finely chopped

- 1 rib celery, finely chopped

- 4 large cloves garlic, chopped
- Coarse salt and pepper
- Two 15-ounce cans cannellini beans
- 1 cup canned tomato sauce or canned crushed tomatoes
- 2 cups water
- 1 quart chicken stock
- 1 1/2 cups ditalini
- Grated Parmigiano or Romano, for the table
- Crusty bread, for mopping

Directions

1. Heat a deep pot over medium high heat and add oil and pancetta. Brown the pancetta bits lightly, and add herb stems, bay leaf, chopped vegetables, and garlic. Season vegetables with salt and pepper. Add beans, tomato sauce, water, and stock to pot and raise heat to high. Bring soup to a rapid boil and add pasta. Reduce heat to medium and cook soup, stirring occasionally, 6 to 8 minutes or until pasta is cooked al dente. Rosemary and thyme leaves will separate from stems as soup cooks. Remove herb stems and bay leaf from soup and place pot on table on a trivet. Let soup rest and begin to cool for a

few minutes. Ladle soup into bowls and top with lots of grated cheese. Pass crusty bread for bowl mopping.

Beef Stir-Fry
Ingredients

- 1 1/2 pounds skirt steak, cut into 4-inch-long pieces, then cut against the grain into 1/4-inch-thick slices
- Salt and freshly ground pepper
- 1/4 cup low-sodium soy sauce
- 1 serrano chile pepper, seeded and finely chopped
- 2 teaspoons sugar
- 2 tablespoons freshly squeezed lime juice (1 to 2 limes)
- 2 tablespoons olive oil
- 2 cloves garlic, grated
- 1 bunch scallions, thinly sliced
- 6 ounces fresh mushrooms, sliced
- 1/4 pound snow peas or green beans
- 1 12-ounce can baby corn, drained
- 1 red bell pepper, thinly sliced (optional)

Directions

1. Season the steak with salt and pepper. In a medium bowl, whisk together the soy sauce, chile pepper, sugar and lime juice until the sugar is dissolved. Add the beef, toss to coat and set aside.

2. In a large skillet over medium-high heat, heat the oil until shimmering, about 1 minute. Add the beef and cook, stirring, until cooked through, 3 to 5 minutes.

3. Remove the beef from the skillet and set aside. Allow the liquid in the pan to reduce until thickened, about 4 minutes. Add the garlic and scallions and cook 1 minute more. Add the mushrooms and cook for 2 to 3 minutes more. Add the snow peas, baby corn and bell pepper and continue cooking until all the vegetables are crisp-tender, about 2 minutes. Return the beef to the skillet and toss to combine.

Gazpacho
Ingredients

- 1 1/2 pounds vine-ripened tomatoes, peeled, seeded and chopped
- Tomato juice
- 1 cup cucumber, peeled, seeded and chopped
- 1/2 cup chopped red bell pepper

- 1/2 cup chopped red onion
- 1 small jalapeno, seeded and minced
- 1 medium garlic clove, minced
- 1/4 cup extra-virgin olive oil
- 1 lime, juiced
- 2 teaspoons balsamic vinegar
- 2 teaspoons Worcestershire sauce
- 1/2 teaspoon toasted, ground cumin
- 1 teaspoon kosher salt
- 1/4 teaspoon freshly ground black pepper
- 2 tablespoons fresh basil leaves, chiffonade

Directions

1. Fill a 6-quart pot halfway full of water, set over high heat and bring to a boil.
2. Make an X with a paring knife on the bottom of the tomatoes. Drop the tomatoes into the boiling water for 15 seconds, remove and transfer to an ice bath and allow to cool until able to handle, approximately 1 minute. Remove and pat dry. Peel, core and seed the tomatoes. When seeding the tomatoes, place the seeds and pulp

into a fine mesh strainer set over a bowl in order to catch the juice. Press as much of the juice through as possible and then add enough bottled tomato juice to bring the total to 1 cup.

3. Place the tomatoes and juice into a large mixing bowl. Add the cucumber, bell pepper, red onion, jalapeno, garlic clove, olive oil, lime juice, balsamic vinegar, Worcestershire, cumin, salt and pepper and stir to combine. Transfer 1 1/2 cups of the mixture to a blender and puree for 15 to 20 seconds on high speed. Return the pureed mixture to the bowl and stir to combine. Cover and chill for 2 hours and up to overnight. Serve with chiffonade of basil.

Green Beans with Lemon and Garlic
Ingredients

- 2 pounds green beans, ends trimmed
- 1 tablespoon extra-virgin olive oil
- 3 tablespoons butter
- 2 large garlic cloves, minced
- 1 teaspoon red pepper flakes
- 1 tablespoon lemon zest
- Salt and freshly ground black pepper

Directions

1. Blanch green beans in a large stock pot of well salted boiling water until bright green in color and tender crisp, roughly 2 minutes. Drain and shock in a bowl of ice water to stop from cooking.

2. Heat a large heavy skillet over medium heat. Add the oil and the butter. Add the garlic and red pepper flakes and saute until fragrant, about 30 seconds. Add the beans and continue to saute until coated in the butter and heated through, about 5 minutes. Add lemon zest and season with salt and pepper.

Healthy Cauliflower Rice
Ingredients

- 1 large head cauliflower, separated into 1-inch florets
- 3 tablespoons olive oil
- 1 medium onion, finely diced
- Kosher salt
- 2 tablespoons fresh parsley leaves, finely chopped
- Juice of 1/2 lemon

Directions

1. Trim the cauliflower florets, cutting away as much stem as possible. In 3 batches, break up the florets into a food processor and pulse until the mixture resembles couscous.

2. Heat the oil in a large skillet over medium-high heat. At the first wisp of smoke from the oil, add the onions, and stir to coat. Continue cooking, stirring frequently, until the onions are golden brown at the edges and have softened, about 8 minutes. Add the cauliflower, and stir to combine. Add 1 teaspoon salt, and continue to cook, stirring frequently, until the cauliflower has softened, 3 to 5 minutes. Remove from the heat.

3. Spoon the cauliflower into a large serving bowl, garnish with the parsley, sprinkle with the lemon juice and season to taste with salt. Serve warm.

Oven "Fries"

Ingredients

- 3 large baking potatoes, cut into 1/4-inch-thick matchsticks
- 2 tablespoons canola oil
- Salt
- Cooking spray

Directions

1. Preheat the oven to 450 degrees. In a large bowl, toss the potatoes with the oil and 1/2 teaspoon salt. Coat a baking sheet with cooking spray and spread the potatoes in a single layer. Bake until golden and crisp, about 35 minutes. Remove the fries with a spatula and season with salt.

Roman-Style Chicken

Ingredients

- 4 skinless chicken breast halves, with ribs
- 2 skinless chicken thighs, with bones
- 1/2 teaspoon salt, plus 1 teaspoon
- 1/2 teaspoon freshly ground black pepper, plus 1 teaspoon
- 1/4 cup olive oil
- 1 red bell pepper, sliced
- 1 yellow bell pepper, sliced
- 3 ounces prosciutto, chopped
- 2 cloves garlic, chopped
- 1 (15-ounce) can diced tomatoes

- 1/2 cup white wine
- 1 tablespoon fresh thyme leaves
- 1 teaspoon fresh oregano leaves
- 1/2 cup chicken stock
- 2 tablespoons capers
- 1/4 cup chopped fresh flat-leaf parsley leaves

Directions

1. Season the chicken with 1/2 teaspoon salt and 1/2 teaspoon pepper. In a heavy, large skillet, heat the olive oil over medium heat. When the oil is hot, cook the chicken until browned on both sides. Remove from the pan and set aside.

2. Keeping the same pan over medium heat, add the peppers and prosciutto and cook until the peppers have browned and the prosciutto is crisp, about 5 minutes. Add the garlic and cook for 1 minute. Add the tomatoes, wine, and herbs. Using a wooden spoon, scrape the browned bits off the bottom of the pan. Return the chicken to the pan, add the stock, and bring the mixture to a boil. Reduce the heat and simmer, covered, until the chicken is cooked through, about 20 to 30 minutes.

3. If serving immediately, add the capers and the parsley. Stir to combine and serve. If making ahead of time, transfer the chicken and sauce to a storage container, cool, and refrigerate. The next day, reheat the chicken to a simmer over medium heat. Stir in the capers and the parsley and serve.

Salmon Baked in Foil
Ingredients

- 4 (5 ounces each) salmon fillets
- 2 teaspoons olive oil plus 2 tablespoons
- Salt and freshly ground black pepper
- 3 tomatoes, chopped, or 1 (14-ounce) can chopped tomatoes, drained
- 2 chopped shallots
- 2 tablespoons fresh lemon juice
- 1 teaspoon dried oregano
- 1 teaspoon dried thyme

Directions

1. Preheat the oven to 400 degrees F.

2. Sprinkle salmon with 2 teaspoons olive oil, salt, and pepper. Stir the tomatoes, shallots, 2 tablespoons of oil, lemon juice, oregano, thyme, salt and pepper in a medium bowl to blend.

3. Place a salmon fillet, oiled side down, atop a sheet of foil. Wrap the ends of the foil to form a spiral shape. Spoon the tomato mixture over the salmon. Fold the sides of the foil over the fish and tomato mixture, covering completely; seal the packets closed. Place the foil packet on a heavy large baking sheet. Repeat until all of the salmon have been individually wrapped in foil and placed on the baking sheet. Bake until the salmon is just cooked through, about 25 minutes. Using a large metal spatula, transfer the foil packets to plates and serve.

One-week sample menu
Below is 1-week sample meal plan using recipes from Noom's app.

This meal plan would not apply to everyone since calorie recommendations are individualized, but it provides a general overview of the foods included from the green, yellow, and red categories.

Monday
Breakfast: raspberry yogurt parfait

Lunch: vegetarian barley soup

Dinner: fennel, orange, and arugula salad

Snack: creamy cucumber and dill salad

Tuesday

Breakfast: banana-ginger smoothie

Lunch: roasted orange tilapia and asparagus

Dinner: mushroom and rice soup

Snack: deviled eggs

Wednesday

Breakfast: vegetable skillet frittata

Lunch: broccoli quinoa pilaf

Dinner: pork lettuce wraps

Snack: homemade yogurt pops

Thursday

Breakfast: egg sandwich

Lunch: chicken and avocado pita pockets

Dinner: pasta with shellfish and mushrooms

Snack: mixed nuts

Friday
Breakfast: spinach-tomato frittata

Lunch: salmon with tabbouleh salad

Dinner: grilled chicken with corn salsa

Snack: chocolate cake

Saturday
Breakfast: banana-apple and nut oatmeal

Lunch: turkey cheddar tacos

Dinner: green bean casserole

Snack: hummus and peppers

Sunday
Breakfast: scrambled egg wrap

Lunch: loaded spinach salad

Dinner: salmon patties with green beans

Snack: cream cheese fruit dip with apples

Conclusion

Noom is a weight loss app that provides access to a health coach and a personalized weight loss plan. Its creators claim that these tools, plus its accurate food calorie counter, can help people reach their individual weight goals.

So far, research suggests that the Noom app can be an effective aid to weight loss. However, the research has not yet compared Noom with other weight loss apps or methods.

People with underlying health conditions should take extra care when using Noom or similar weight loss apps. Such people may require the advice of a doctor or dietitian to ensure safe weight loss.

Made in the USA
Monee, IL
02 December 2021